THIS JOURNAL BELONGS TO

_____

www.theagilitychallenge.com

THE AGILITY CHALLENGE
PURPOSEFUL PRACTICE DOG AGILITY
TRAINING JOURNAL

Copyright © 2020 Daisy Peel
Written and edited by Daisy Peel
ISBN 978-1-7362115-3-3

All rights reserved. Printed in the United States of America. No part of this book may be used or reproduced in any form or by any means electronic or mechanical, including photocopying, recording, or by any information storage or retrieval system, without the prior written permission of the author, except in the case of brief quotations embodied in critical articles and reviews and certain other noncommercial uses permitted by copyright law. For permission requests, write to Daisy Peel at daisy@daisypeel.com.

Trademarks: All service marks, trademarks, and product names used int his publication belong to their respective holders.

This book is available at special quantity discounts for club promotions, premiums, or educational use. Write for details.

If you'd like to share this journal with others, please do so by directing them to **https://www.theagilitychallenge.com**!

First edition
First printing December 2020

PURPOSEFUL PRACTICE
DOG AGILITY
TRAINING JOURNAL

BY
DAISY PEEL

LEARN MORE AT
WWW.THEAGILITYCHALLENGE.COM

About The Author

Daisy Peel is known worldwide as a leading instructor and competitor in the sport of dog agility. She has represented the USA internationally over a dozen times, across three continents, with four different dogs.

Daisy is recognized worldwide for her abilities as an instructor. She is a formally trained teacher, with a degree in science and math education, and was a high school chemistry teacher for nearly a decade before becoming a full time dog agility coach and instructor. Daisy's students have excelled at the top levels in AKC, USDAA, AAC (Canada), and UKI, and have themselves been selected to represent their countries at international events.

Daisy is dedicated to the improvement of handlers at all levels, regardless of their current level or goals and aspirations. She teaches students of all ages & stages around the globe, in person and through her online classes, and is dedicated to helping people further their self-improvement through better training, better handling, and better mastery of their mental game.

Daisy has been on the forefront of the trend of online agility education, and her online program **The Agility Challenge** is one of the leading sources for those seeking to improve the quality of their participation in the sport from afar. Her instruction, whether online or in person, is widely sought after as some of the best instruction available for those at any level, with any type of dog.

To learn more about Daisy and what she has to offer in terms of online instruction, visit her website at:
www.daisypeel.com

Or take a look at her online program The Agility Challenge, which this journal was developed for, at:
www.theagilitychallenge.com

TABLE OF CONTENTS

PAGE	TOPIC
1	Forward And Introduction
7	How To Use This Journal
11	Monthly Tracking & Planning
25	Pre & Post Event Goal Setting & Tracking
69	Training Session Tracking Sheets
282	To Do Lists

TABLE OF CONTENTS

PAGE	TOPIC

TABLE OF CONTENTS

PAGE	TOPIC

TABLE OF CONTENTS

PAGE	TOPIC

TABLE OF CONTENTS

PAGE	TOPIC

TABLE OF CONTENTS

PAGE	TOPIC

Forward & Introduction

Welcome to **The Agility Challenge Purposeful Practice Dog Agility Training Journal**! This journal was developed to help you effectively incorporate the elements of ***deliberate practice*** into your training and practice. It includes forms and logs that I use in my own training to make sure that I maximize my time and enjoyment with my dogs. I love to train, but I also love to make progress on my training and handling goals, and deliberate, purposeful practice has been an absolute game changer for me over the years!

What is deliberate practice? Of course, dog agility is our time to play with our dogs, but author and researcher K. Anders Ericsson defines deliberate practice as *"a highly structured activity, the explicit goal of which is to improve performance*[1]*."*

What Does Deliberate Practice Look Like?

In deliberate practice, as opposed to simply playing or spending time with your dog, specific tasks are invented to overcome weaknesses, and performance is carefully monitored to provide cues for ways to improve it further. Deliberate practice requires effort and may not be inherently enjoyable - although we should always work to make sure our dogs are having a great time, we may have to step way out of our own comfort zones to overcome training and handling obstacles that stand in our way.

> *Deliberate practice is a highly structured activity, the explicit goal of which is to improve performance*

We need to be ok with operating outside our comfort zone to improve our training and handling, and the training and handling of our dog. Great handlers and trainers are motivated to practice because they know that practice improves performance! Get on the edges of your comfort zone for maximum improvement!

Engaging in deliberate practice generates no immediate monetary rewards and generates costs associated with access to teachers and training environments. Nobody is paying you to practice - in fact, you're spending a lot of time and money going to classes, private lessons with your trainer, consuming information about training and handling, paying for rental or practice time on equipment, and paying for entries to shows!

It's Not Work, And It's Not Play

Deliberate practice isn't work, but it's not play, either. Sure, there are days when we just want to play with our dogs, and that's fine. But *"just playing with our dogs"* should not be confused with deliberate practice to improve our skills, or our dog's skills. When we're engaged in deliberate practice, we're engaged in activities designed to stretch us, that require our total focus. These activities stretch our dogs and require *their* focus as well!

Setting aside time to play with our dogs is critical. Taking the time to enjoy the skills that we possess as a team, those things we've already worked hard for that are on 'auto-pilot' is the reward for all of our deliberate practice. However, to realize maximum benefit from our training, we must be purposeful, have a plan, stay focused, be precise, and be persistent.

How Can I Do This Better?

This is the question that should be asked, each and every time you train or practice, if you're engaging in **deliberate practice**. Rather than heading out with your dog to do the things you are already good at, you'll select an activity from a list of activities that you know you and your dog need to work on (skills you don't currently possess or are weak at). Then, you'll target that skill in your training.

To realize maximum benefit from our training, we must be purposeful, have a plan, stay focused, be precise, and be persistent

---

For Every Training Session:

1. You need to establish a (reachable) **specific goal**. Vague overall performance targets like 'succeed' or 'get better' won't cut it. *Write down your goal for each training session in this journal before heading out to train!*

2. You must be maximally **focused** on improvement during practice. It must be intense, uninterrupted and at least somewhat repetitive ('drilling'). Not always particularly pleasant, but highly rewarding. It's also critical that you make deliberate practice rewarding for your dog, which means you will potentially need to break things down in to very small and rewardable pieces that you can repeat for additional reinforcement!

3. You must receive **immediate feedback** on your performance. Without it, you can't figure out what you need to modify or how close you are to achieving your specific goal. Luckily, although many of us train alone, we always have our dog available to give us that immediate feedback!

4. You must **get out of your comfort zone**, constantly attempting things that are just out of reach. Ideally, you'll feel uncomfortable - *the whole time*.

A hallmark of deliberate practice is that performance level during training is not initially at the desired level – there is a gap. **By the end of each training session, there should be something measurable that you or your dog has improved on.**

Embracing these principles in training squeezes the trigger of the greatest weapon in the arsenal of the human brain – adaptability.

Every training session should be viewed as a challenge to refine and improve.

---

1. The Role of Deliberate Practice in the Acquisition of Expert Performance. K. Anders Ericsson , Ralf Th. Krampe, and Clemens Tesch-Römer. Psychological Review, 1993, Vol 100 No. 3 363-406

A Deliberate Practice Session Example

Goal: 80% success rate with dog-on-left weave entries with four poles, from straight on approaches to 90° approaches.

Focus: Reread weave pole training articles or talk to my trainer for a plan, then warm up my dog, play, and work on dog-on-left weave entries, starting at 0° and working toward 90°, rewarding for each successful entry, and withholding reinforcement for each unsuccessful entry. At the end of 10 attempts, play with my dog, and put her in her kennel to evaluate the session.

Feedback: Keep track of the number of attempts, number of successes, and number of failures, as well as approximate angles of approach. Analyze success rate at each angle and work on unsuccessful angles in the next 10-rep session.

Exit comfort zone: Repeat the 10-repetition sessions three more times for a total of four 10-rep sessions. Each time, work on the unsuccessful angles from the previous session, rewarding for success. Be sure to avoid 'helping' your dog by stepping in and changing the angle of approach.

How To Use This Journal

This journal is made to be written in! Keeping track of your training sessions is key to remaining mindful and deliberate about what you're doing. If it's worth doing, it's worth writing down!

The notes you made during the previous training session, along with the items on your To Do List (at the back of this journal) will guide subsequent training sessions. Draw pictures, make lists, write paragraphs or cryptic shorthand notes - it's entirely up to you how to populate the pages of this journal, although I do have a few suggestions to help get you started on the next page.

Keeping track of your training sessions is key to remaining mindful and deliberate about what you're doing

Over the course of several sessions, you'll be able to see whether or not you're making progress with your chosen plan of attack on any particular training topic. You'll also be able to see if maybe you've been obsessing on on topic or skill to the exclusion of others that need to be addressed.

If you run in to a training situation that you don't know how to solve, make a note in your journal, and ask your trainer, coach, mentor, or a friend for help formulating and implementing a solution!

Suggestions for each journal entry

The entry forms in this journal allow you to keep track of the following:

- The date and time of day (morning, afternoon, etc.)
- What you worked on and what your criteria for success for the session was, and whether or not you met those criteria. Does the topic warrant further training? Are there questions about this topic that you have that you'd like input on?
- Whether or not you approached the session with the mindset of engaging in deliberate, purposeful practice.
  - Were you engaged, mindful, and present for your dog?
  - Did you have a clear picture of what you wanted to work on and why?
  - Were you working on a skill that either you or your dog needed to improve on, or were you simply enjoying the skills you and your dog are already proficient at?
  - Were you on the edge of your comfort zone?

- A brief note on whether or not you need to work on the same topic during the next session, and what criteria you'll be aiming for.
- Use the star system in this journal to rate each training session according to the questions above.
  - A 4-star training session means that either I or my dog was at the edge of our comfort zone with respect to the skill worked on, that I tackled it purposefully, and that I made some concrete, observable progress with respect to our proficiency with the skill.
  - A 1-star training session might be very enjoyable, but with no real purpose. Or, we may have been working on a skill we were not proficient at, but with no real focus and no real plan for improvement. Or, maybe I had a plan, but that plan very quickly revealed itself to not be appropriate for me or my dog, and reevaluation is required prior to the next session. Or, maybe I was grumpy, hungry, dehydrated, or just not present for my dog for some reason (and in that case, I'll try to note why so I can avoid that in the future!).

Your To Do List

At the back of this journal I have provided space for you to keep a "To Do List." Every time you find a weakness or a gap, write it down on your To Do List so that you can remember to address it in training at some point! If a friend has trained their dog to do something neat, and you'd like to train your dog to do that as well, put it on your To Do List! If you or your dog encounter something at a competition that you haven't seen before, put it on your To Do List!

Your To Do List will help shape future training sessions, as well as help keep you honest. If you and your dog keep having difficulty with a particular skill on course, and that skill is on your list, but you haven't worked on it in training, then an opportunity for deliberate practice on that topic has presented itself!

If you have something on your To Do List but don't have a plan for how to address it in training, ask your coach, instructor, mentor, or friend to help you out!

MONTHLY TRACKING & PLANNING

On the following pages, you'll find monthly tracking sheets for each month of the year. Use these monthly tracking sheets to keep a log of your activity over the course of the month. This log is a brief overview, and it can help you keep track of how often you're working on a training topic. It will also help you keep track of how long it's been since you've worked on an important training topic!

With dog training, it's important to strike a balance. Too easily, we can obsess on a training topic we're having trouble with, and ignore other training topics that need our attention. For example, if you work on weave poles every day of the month, but then look back and note that you've only worked on your dog's seesaw performance once in the past month, it will be no surprise that your dog has fantastic weave poles, but a weak seesaw performance! It's important to cycle regularly through ALL of the items on your training to-do list, and the Monthly Tracking & Planning logs can help with this.

These logs aren't just for tracking. They're good for planning as well. Take a few minutes at the beginning of each month and write down a list of topics you'd like to address, in the leftmost column. In parenthesis, make a note of how many days of each month you'd like to work on that topic. Then, put a tick in the box for each day that you actually work on that topic. Or, if you like, put the page number that you logged this training session in the box, under the date you worked on the topic, so you can easily refer to the training session! An example is below for you to take a look at.

You can see that I met some of my monthly goals in terms of how often I wanted to work on a given topic, and that I referred to the page in my journal where I logged the training session, so I could look at the details later.

MONTHLY TRACKING & PLANNING FOR THE MONTH OF: January

	1	2	3	4	5	6	7	8	9	10	11	12	13	14	15	16	17	18	19	20	21	22	23	24	25	26	27	28	29	30	31
Weaves (10)		15			20				24			26			27		28			29		30		31							
Seesaw (5)		15			20		23			25					28																
Start Line Stays (15)		15			20		23		24				27				29						33	34	35	36					
Jumping (10)	15	16	20	21	23								27		28		29		30		31										

MONTHLY TRACKING & PLANNING FOR THE MONTH OF:

1	2	3	4	5	6	7	8	9	10	11	12	13	14	15	16	17	18	19	20	21	22	23	24	25	26	27	28	29	30	31

MONTHLY TRACKING & PLANNING FOR THE MONTH OF:

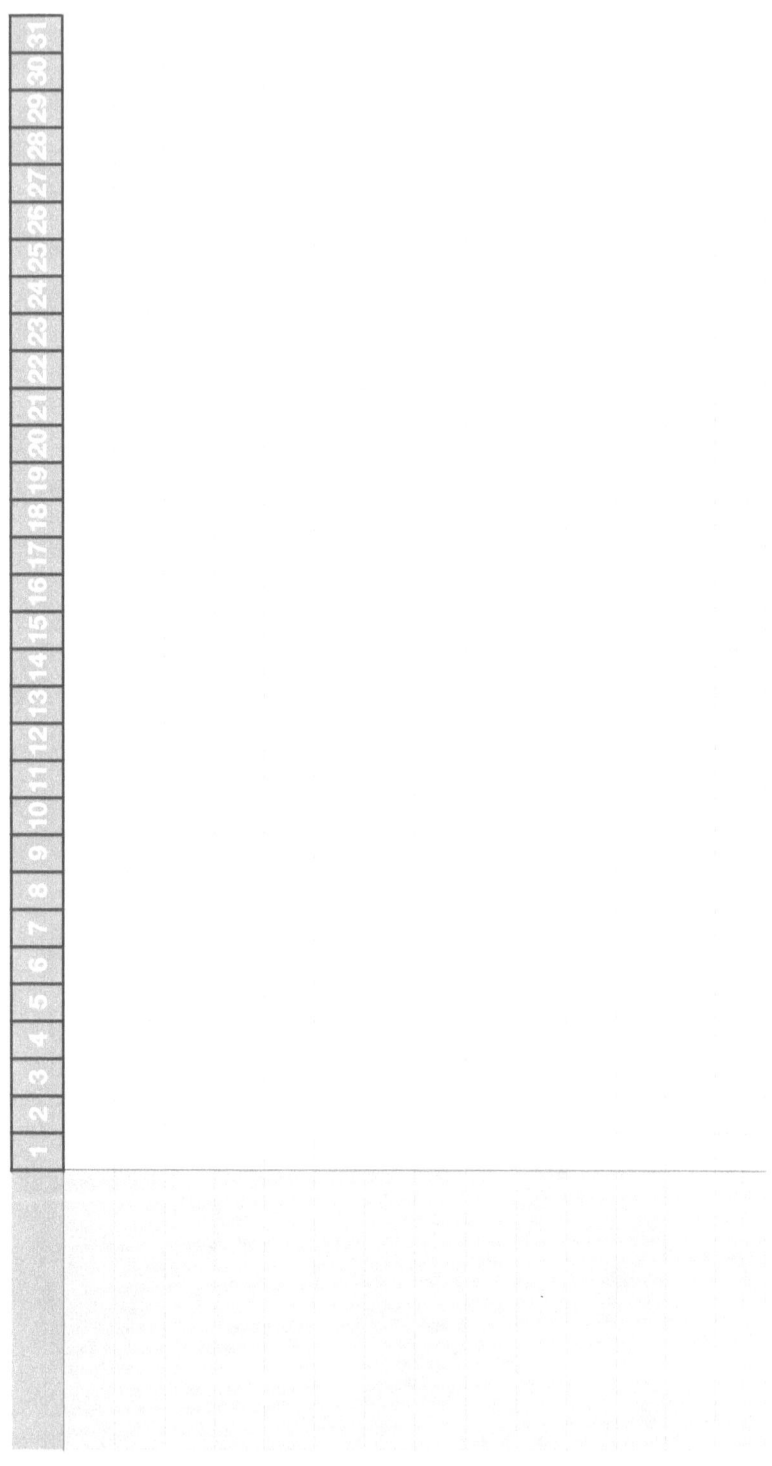

MONTHLY TRACKING & PLANNING FOR THE MONTH OF:

1	2	3	4	5	6	7	8	9	10	11	12	13	14	15	16	17	18	19	20	21	22	23	24	25	26	27	28	29	30	31

MONTHLY TRACKING & PLANNING FOR THE MONTH OF:

MONTHLY TRACKING & PLANNING FOR THE MONTH OF:

	1	2	3	4	5	6	7	8	9	10	11	12	13	14	15	16	17	18	19	20	21	22	23	24	25	26	27	28	29	30	31

MONTHLY TRACKING & PLANNING FOR THE MONTH OF:

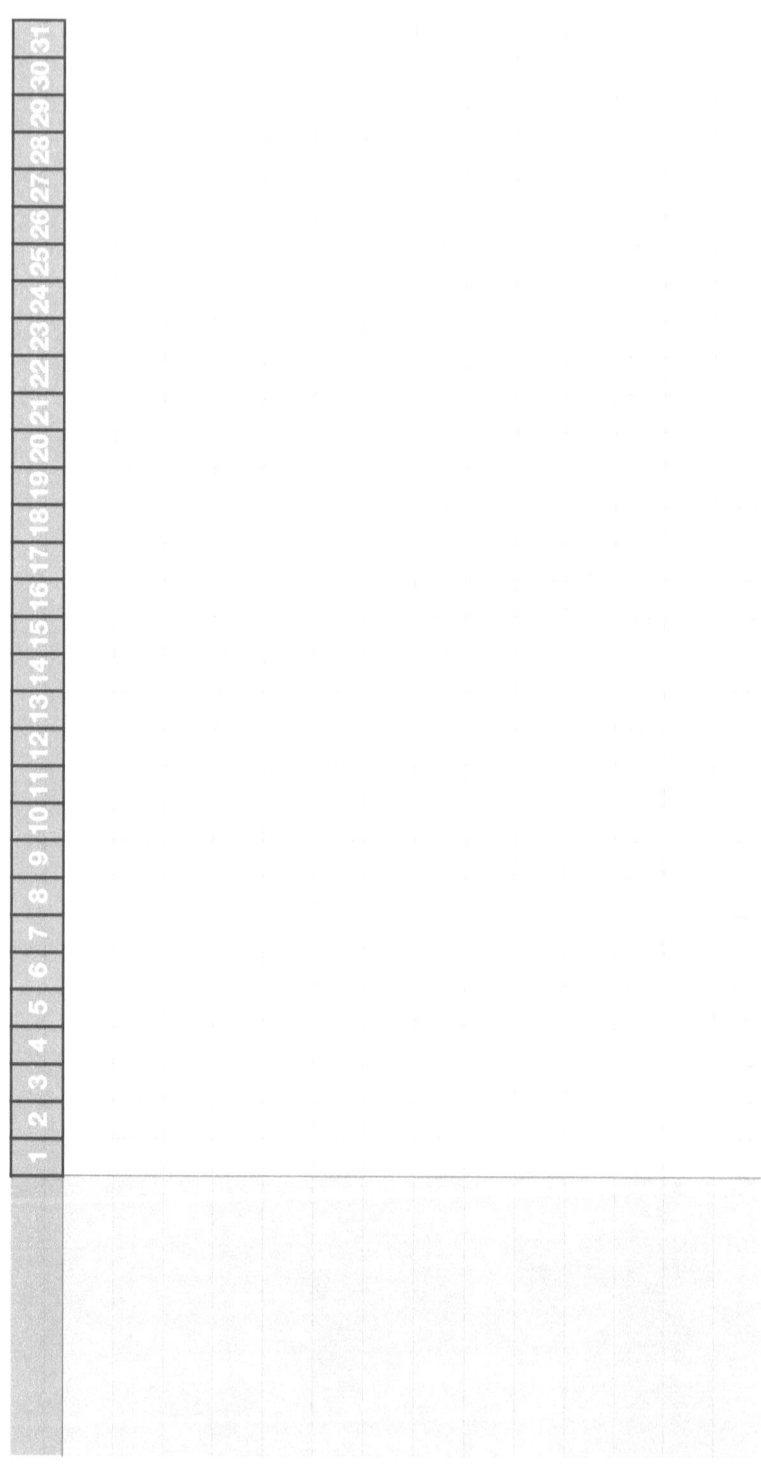

MONTHLY TRACKING & PLANNING FOR THE MONTH OF:

1	2	3	4	5	6	7	8	9	10	11	12	13	14	15	16	17	18	19	20	21	22	23	24	25	26	27	28	29	30	31

MONTHLY TRACKING & PLANNING FOR THE MONTH OF:

1	2	3	4	5	6	7	8	9	10	11	12	13	14	15	16	17	18	19	20	21	22	23	24	25	26	27	28	29	30	31

MONTHLY TRACKING & PLANNING FOR THE MONTH OF:

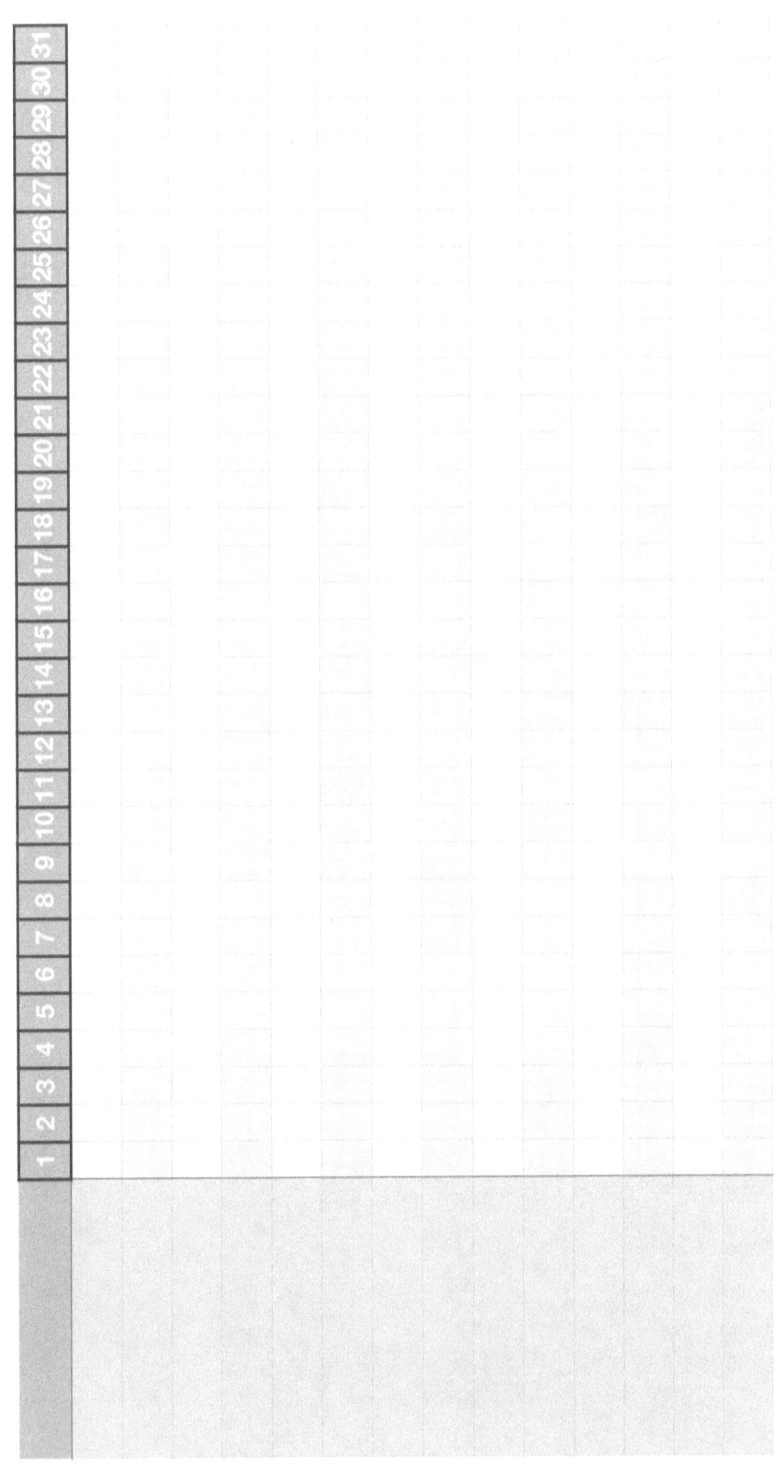

MONTHLY TRACKING & PLANNING FOR THE MONTH OF:

1	2	3	4	5	6	7	8	9	10	11	12	13	14	15	16	17	18	19	20	21	22	23	24	25	26	27	28	29	30	31

MONTHLY TRACKING & PLANNING FOR THE MONTH OF:

MONTHLY TRACKING & PLANNING FOR THE MONTH OF:

1	2	3	4	5	6	7	8	9	10	11	12	13	14	15	16	17	18	19	20	21	22	23	24	25	26	27	28	29	30	31

PRE & POST EVENT GOAL SETTING & TRACKING

Setting goals related specifically to an event (fun match, League, competition, etc.) will help you stay focused and in the right mindset. Taking the time to reflect on how you and your dog did with respect to your pre-event planning after the event is over will help you keep track of your successes and give you direction when planning for the future.

I use the following worksheets before competitions, large and small, as well as prior to seminars and workshops. Being in the right mindset is key to being deliberate and purposeful with your practice and training. It's also crucial to get in to the right mindset if you're going to be spending time in a learning environment. Although you are the leader and instructor for your dog, you also have to, at the same time, be a learner and student.

You'll need to be able to be coachable - to listen and act on feedback, even while you're asking your dog to do the same for you. This is no small task! I give these worksheets out to members of The Agility Challenge to use for their own personal record keeping and reflection, and I also give them out to my students, and to those who will be attending my workshops and seminars.

It's important to know what your personal performance as well as mindset goals are, going in to a competition or event. The following worksheets will help you stay on track with your mindset. I encourage you to use these worksheets to help gain clarity about your mindset goals going in to new situations, or, in to situations that have historically been problematic for you in terms of mindset, focus, anxiety, etc.

I also encourage students, workshop participants, and attendees to use these forms when working with a coach, instructor, or mentor, so that the person who is helping you with your dog training can gain some insight in to where you may be having trouble with your focus and mindset. As with your training, being purposeful and deliberate about your mindset pays off!

Event Date/s:

Event Name and Type:

Event Location:

Dog/s Entered:

PRE EVENT PLANNING
What are your performance goals, for you & your dog?

_____

_____

_____

_____

_____

What are your mindset & focus goals for this event?

_____

_____

_____

_____

_____

POST EVENT EVALUATION & REFLECTION
Did YOU meet your performance goals for this event?
What skills were stronger than you anticipated? What skills were weaker than you anticipated? What helped or hindered your performance at this event *that you have control over & can improve upon?*

_____

_____

_____

Did your DOG meet your performance goals for this event?
Evaluate whether or not your dog met your performance goals for this event. What skills were stronger than you anticipated? What skills were weaker than you anticipated? What helped or hindered your dog's performance at this event *that you have control over and can improve upon?*

Did YOU meet your mindset & focus goals for this event?
Were you more or less focused and mindful than you anticipated? What helped or hindered your state of mind at this event *that you have control over and can improve upon?*

Event Date/s:

Event Name and Type:

Event Location:

Dog/s Entered:

PRE EVENT PLANNING
What are your performance goals, for you & your dog?

_____
_____
_____
_____
_____

What are your mindset & focus goals for this event?

_____
_____
_____
_____
_____

POST EVENT EVALUATION & REFLECTION
Did YOU meet your performance goals for this event?
What skills were stronger than you anticipated? What skills were weaker than you anticipated? What helped or hindered your performance at this event *that you have control over & can improve upon?*

_____
_____
_____

Did your DOG meet your performance goals for this event?
Evaluate whether or not your dog met your performance goals for this event. What skills were stronger than you anticipated? What skills were weaker than you anticipated? What helped or hindered your dog's performance at this event *that you have control over and can improve upon?*

Did YOU meet your mindset & focus goals for this event?
Were you more or less focused and mindful than you anticipated? What helped or hindered your state of mind at this event *that you have control over and can improve upon?*

Event Date/s:

Event Name and Type:

Event Location:

Dog/s Entered:

PRE EVENT PLANNING
What are your performance goals, for you & your dog?

_____

_____

_____

_____

_____

What are your mindset & focus goals for this event?

_____

_____

_____

_____

_____

POST EVENT EVALUATION & REFLECTION
Did YOU meet your performance goals for this event?
What skills were stronger than you anticipated? What skills were weaker than you anticipated? What helped or hindered your performance at this event *that you have control over & can improve upon?*

_____

_____

_____

_____

_____

_____

_____

Did your DOG meet your performance goals for this event?
Evaluate whether or not your dog met your performance goals for this event. What skills were stronger than you anticipated? What skills were weaker than you anticipated? What helped or hindered your dog's performance at this event *that you have control over and can improve upon?*

_____

_____

_____

_____

_____

_____

_____

Did YOU meet your mindset & focus goals for this event?
Were you more or less focused and mindful than you anticipated? What helped or hindered your state of mind at this event *that you have control over and can improve upon?*

_____

_____

_____

_____

_____

_____

Event Date/s:

Event Name and Type:

Event Location:

Dog/s Entered:

PRE EVENT PLANNING
What are your performance goals, for you & your dog?

_____

_____

_____

_____

_____

What are your mindset & focus goals for this event?

_____

_____

_____

_____

_____

POST EVENT EVALUATION & REFLECTION
Did YOU meet your performance goals for this event?
What skills were stronger than you anticipated? What skills were weaker than you anticipated? What helped or hindered your performance at this event *that you have control over & can improve upon?*

_____

_____

_____

_____
_____
_____
_____

Did your DOG meet your performance goals for this event?

Evaluate whether or not your dog met your performance goals for this event. What skills were stronger than you anticipated? What skills were weaker than you anticipated? What helped or hindered your dog's performance at this event ***that you have control over and can improve upon?***

_____
_____
_____
_____
_____
_____

Did YOU meet your mindset & focus goals for this event?

Were you more or less focused and mindful than you anticipated? What helped or hindered your state of mind at this event ***that you have control over and can improve upon?***

_____
_____
_____
_____
_____

Event Date/s:

Event Name and Type:

Event Location:

Dog/s Entered:

PRE EVENT PLANNING
What are your performance goals, for you & your dog?

_____
_____
_____
_____
_____

What are your mindset & focus goals for this event?

_____
_____
_____
_____
_____

POST EVENT EVALUATION & REFLECTION
Did YOU meet your performance goals for this event?
What skills were stronger than you anticipated? What skills were weaker than you anticipated? What helped or hindered your performance at this event *that you have control over & can improve upon?*

_____
_____
_____

_____

_____

_____

_____

Did your DOG meet your performance goals for this event?
Evaluate whether or not your dog met your performance goals for this event. What skills were stronger than you anticipated? What skills were weaker than you anticipated? What helped or hindered your dog's performance at this event *that you have control over and can improve upon?*

_____

_____

_____

_____

_____

_____

Did YOU meet your mindset & focus goals for this event?
Were you more or less focused and mindful than you anticipated? What helped or hindered your state of mind at this event *that you have control over and can improve upon?*

_____

_____

_____

_____

_____

Event Date/s:

Event Name and Type:

Event Location:

Dog/s Entered:

PRE EVENT PLANNING
What are your performance goals, for you & your dog?

_____

_____

_____

_____

_____

What are your mindset & focus goals for this event?

_____

_____

_____

_____

_____

POST EVENT EVALUATION & REFLECTION
Did YOU meet your performance goals for this event?
What skills were stronger than you anticipated? What skills were weaker than you anticipated? What helped or hindered your performance at this event *that you have control over & can improve upon?*

_____

_____

_____

_____

_____

_____

_____

Did your DOG meet your performance goals for this event?
Evaluate whether or not your dog met your performance goals for this event. What skills were stronger than you anticipated? What skills were weaker than you anticipated? What helped or hindered your dog's performance at this event *that you have control over and can improve upon?*

_____

_____

_____

_____

_____

_____

Did YOU meet your mindset & focus goals for this event?
Were you more or less focused and mindful than you anticipated? What helped or hindered your state of mind at this event *that you have control over and can improve upon?*

_____

_____

_____

_____

_____

Event Date/s:

Event Name and Type:

Event Location:

Dog/s Entered:

PRE EVENT PLANNING

What are your performance goals, for you & your dog?

_____

_____

_____

_____

_____

What are your mindset & focus goals for this event?

_____

_____

_____

_____

_____

POST EVENT EVALUATION & REFLECTION

Did YOU meet your performance goals for this event?
What skills were stronger than you anticipated? What skills were weaker than you anticipated? What helped or hindered your performance at this event *that you have control over & can improve upon?*

_____

_____

_____

_____

_____

_____

_____

Did your DOG meet your performance goals for this event?
Evaluate whether or not your dog met your performance goals for this event. What skills were stronger than you anticipated? What skills were weaker than you anticipated? What helped or hindered your dog's performance at this event *that you have control over and can improve upon?*

_____

_____

_____

_____

_____

_____

Did YOU meet your mindset & focus goals for this event?
Were you more or less focused and mindful than you anticipated? What helped or hindered your state of mind at this event *that you have control over and can improve upon?*

_____

_____

_____

_____

_____

Event Date/s:

Event Name and Type:

Event Location:

Dog/s Entered:

PRE EVENT PLANNING
What are your performance goals, for you & your dog?

_____
_____
_____
_____
_____
_____

What are your mindset & focus goals for this event?

_____
_____
_____
_____
_____
_____

POST EVENT EVALUATION & REFLECTION
Did YOU meet your performance goals for this event?
What skills were stronger than you anticipated? What skills were weaker than you anticipated? What helped or hindered your performance at this event *that you have control over & can improve upon?*

_____
_____
_____

Did your DOG meet your performance goals for this event?
Evaluate whether or not your dog met your performance goals for this event. What skills were stronger than you anticipated? What skills were weaker than you anticipated? What helped or hindered your dog's performance at this event *that you have control over and can improve upon?*

Did YOU meet your mindset & focus goals for this event?
Were you more or less focused and mindful than you anticipated? What helped or hindered your state of mind at this event *that you have control over and can improve upon?*

Event Date/s:

Event Name and Type:

Event Location:

Dog/s Entered:

PRE EVENT PLANNING
What are your performance goals, for you & your dog?

_____

_____

_____

_____

_____

What are your mindset & focus goals for this event?

_____

_____

_____

_____

_____

POST EVENT EVALUATION & REFLECTION
Did YOU meet your performance goals for this event?
What skills were stronger than you anticipated? What skills were weaker than you anticipated? What helped or hindered your performance at this event *that you have control over & can improve upon?*

_____

_____

_____

Did your DOG meet your performance goals for this event?
Evaluate whether or not your dog met your performance goals for this event. What skills were stronger than you anticipated? What skills were weaker than you anticipated? What helped or hindered your dog's performance at this event *that you have control over and can improve upon?*

Did YOU meet your mindset & focus goals for this event?
Were you more or less focused and mindful than you anticipated? What helped or hindered your state of mind at this event *that you have control over and can improve upon?*

Event Date/s:

Event Name and Type:

Event Location:

Dog/s Entered:

PRE EVENT PLANNING
What are your performance goals, for you & your dog?

_____

_____

_____

_____

_____

What are your mindset & focus goals for this event?

_____

_____

_____

_____

_____

POST EVENT EVALUATION & REFLECTION
Did YOU meet your performance goals for this event?
What skills were stronger than you anticipated? What skills were weaker than you anticipated? What helped or hindered your performance at this event *that you have control over & can improve upon?*

_____

_____

_____

_____

_____

_____

_____

Did your DOG meet your performance goals for this event?
Evaluate whether or not your dog met your performance goals for this event. What skills were stronger than you anticipated? What skills were weaker than you anticipated? What helped or hindered your dog's performance at this event *that you have control over and can improve upon?*

_____

_____

_____

_____

_____

_____

Did YOU meet your mindset & focus goals for this event?
Were you more or less focused and mindful than you anticipated? What helped or hindered your state of mind at this event *that you have control over and can improve upon?*

_____

_____

_____

_____

_____

Event Date/s:

Event Name and Type:

Event Location:

Dog/s Entered:

PRE EVENT PLANNING
What are your performance goals, for you & your dog?

_____
_____
_____
_____
_____

What are your mindset & focus goals for this event?

_____
_____
_____
_____
_____

POST EVENT EVALUATION & REFLECTION
Did YOU meet your performance goals for this event?
What skills were stronger than you anticipated? What skills were weaker than you anticipated? What helped or hindered your performance at this event *that you have control over & can improve upon?*

_____
_____
_____

_____

_____

_____

_____

Did your DOG meet your performance goals for this event?
Evaluate whether or not your dog met your performance goals for this event. What skills were stronger than you anticipated? What skills were weaker than you anticipated? What helped or hindered your dog's performance at this event *that you have control over and can improve upon?*

_____

_____

_____

_____

_____

_____

Did YOU meet your mindset & focus goals for this event?
Were you more or less focused and mindful than you anticipated? What helped or hindered your state of mind at this event *that you have control over and can improve upon?*

_____

_____

_____

_____

_____

Event Date/s:

Event Name and Type:

Event Location:

Dog/s Entered:

PRE EVENT PLANNING
What are your performance goals, for you & your dog?

_____

_____

_____

_____

_____

_____

What are your mindset & focus goals for this event?

_____

_____

_____

_____

_____

_____

POST EVENT EVALUATION & REFLECTION
Did YOU meet your performance goals for this event?
What skills were stronger than you anticipated? What skills were weaker than you anticipated? What helped or hindered your performance at this event *that you have control over & can improve upon?*

_____

_____

_____

_____

_____

_____

_____

Did your DOG meet your performance goals for this event?
Evaluate whether or not your dog met your performance goals for this event. What skills were stronger than you anticipated? What skills were weaker than you anticipated? What helped or hindered your dog's performance at this event *that you have control over and can improve upon?*

_____

_____

_____

_____

_____

_____

Did YOU meet your mindset & focus goals for this event?
Were you more or less focused and mindful than you anticipated? What helped or hindered your state of mind at this event *that you have control over and can improve upon?*

_____

_____

_____

_____

_____

Event Date/s:

Event Name and Type:

Event Location:

Dog/s Entered:

PRE EVENT PLANNING

What are your performance goals, for you & your dog?

_____

_____

_____

_____

_____

What are your mindset & focus goals for this event?

_____

_____

_____

_____

_____

POST EVENT EVALUATION & REFLECTION

Did YOU meet your performance goals for this event?
What skills were stronger than you anticipated? What skills were weaker than you anticipated? What helped or hindered your performance at this event *that you have control over & can improve upon?*

_____

_____

_____

Did your DOG meet your performance goals for this event?
Evaluate whether or not your dog met your performance goals for this event. What skills were stronger than you anticipated? What skills were weaker than you anticipated? What helped or hindered your dog's performance at this event *that you have control over and can improve upon?*

Did YOU meet your mindset & focus goals for this event?
Were you more or less focused and mindful than you anticipated? What helped or hindered your state of mind at this event *that you have control over and can improve upon?*

Event Date/s:

Event Name and Type:

Event Location:

Dog/s Entered:

PRE EVENT PLANNING
What are your performance goals, for you & your dog?

_____

_____

_____

_____

_____

What are your mindset & focus goals for this event?

_____

_____

_____

_____

_____

POST EVENT EVALUATION & REFLECTION
Did YOU meet your performance goals for this event?
What skills were stronger than you anticipated? What skills were weaker than you anticipated? What helped or hindered your performance at this event *that you have control over & can improve upon?*

_____

_____

_____

_____

_____

_____

_____

Did your DOG meet your performance goals for this event?
Evaluate whether or not your dog met your performance goals for this event. What skills were stronger than you anticipated? What skills were weaker than you anticipated? What helped or hindered your dog's performance at this event *that you have control over and can improve upon?*

_____

_____

_____

_____

_____

_____

Did YOU meet your mindset & focus goals for this event?
Were you more or less focused and mindful than you anticipated? What helped or hindered your state of mind at this event *that you have control over and can improve upon?*

_____

_____

_____

_____

_____

Event Date/s:

Event Name and Type:

Event Location:

Dog/s Entered:

PRE EVENT PLANNING
What are your performance goals, for you & your dog?

_____

_____

_____

_____

_____

What are your mindset & focus goals for this event?

_____

_____

_____

_____

_____

POST EVENT EVALUATION & REFLECTION
Did YOU meet your performance goals for this event?
What skills were stronger than you anticipated? What skills were weaker than you anticipated? What helped or hindered your performance at this event *that you have control over & can improve upon?*

_____

_____

_____

_____

_____

_____

_____

Did your DOG meet your performance goals for this event?
Evaluate whether or not your dog met your performance goals for this event. What skills were stronger than you anticipated? What skills were weaker than you anticipated? What helped or hindered your dog's performance at this event *that you have control over and can improve upon?*

_____

_____

_____

_____

_____

_____

Did YOU meet your mindset & focus goals for this event?
Were you more or less focused and mindful than you anticipated? What helped or hindered your state of mind at this event *that you have control over and can improve upon?*

_____

_____

_____

_____

_____

Event Date/s:

Event Name and Type:

Event Location:

Dog/s Entered:

PRE EVENT PLANNING
What are your performance goals, for you & your dog?

_____

_____

_____

_____

_____

What are your mindset & focus goals for this event?

_____

_____

_____

_____

_____

POST EVENT EVALUATION & REFLECTION
Did YOU meet your performance goals for this event?
What skills were stronger than you anticipated? What skills were weaker than you anticipated? What helped or hindered your performance at this event *that you have control over & can improve upon?*

_____

_____

_____

_____

_____

_____

_____

Did your DOG meet your performance goals for this event?
Evaluate whether or not your dog met your performance goals for this event. What skills were stronger than you anticipated? What skills were weaker than you anticipated? What helped or hindered your dog's performance at this event *that you have control over and can improve upon?*

_____

_____

_____

_____

_____

_____

Did YOU meet your mindset & focus goals for this event?
Were you more or less focused and mindful than you anticipated? What helped or hindered your state of mind at this event *that you have control over and can improve upon?*

_____

_____

_____

_____

_____

Event Date/s:

Event Name and Type:

Event Location:

Dog/s Entered:

PRE EVENT PLANNING
What are your performance goals, for you & your dog?

___

___

___

___

___

What are your mindset & focus goals for this event?

___

___

___

___

___

POST EVENT EVALUATION & REFLECTION
Did YOU meet your performance goals for this event?
What skills were stronger than you anticipated? What skills were weaker than you anticipated? What helped or hindered your performance at this event *that you have control over & can improve upon?*

___

___

___

_____
_____
_____
_____

Did your DOG meet your performance goals for this event?
Evaluate whether or not your dog met your performance goals for this event. What skills were stronger than you anticipated? What skills were weaker than you anticipated? What helped or hindered your dog's performance at this event *that you have control over and can improve upon?*

_____
_____
_____
_____
_____
_____

Did YOU meet your mindset & focus goals for this event?
Were you more or less focused and mindful than you anticipated? What helped or hindered your state of mind at this event *that you have control over and can improve upon?*

_____
_____
_____
_____
_____

Event Date/s:

Event Name and Type:

Event Location:

Dog/s Entered:

PRE EVENT PLANNING
What are your performance goals, for you & your dog?

_____
_____
_____
_____
_____

What are your mindset & focus goals for this event?

_____
_____
_____
_____
_____

POST EVENT EVALUATION & REFLECTION
Did YOU meet your performance goals for this event?
What skills were stronger than you anticipated? What skills were weaker than you anticipated? What helped or hindered your performance at this event *that you have control over & can improve upon?*

_____
_____
_____

_____

_____

_____

_____

Did your DOG meet your performance goals for this event?
Evaluate whether or not your dog met your performance goals for this event. What skills were stronger than you anticipated? What skills were weaker than you anticipated? What helped or hindered your dog's performance at this event *that you have control over and can improve upon?*

_____

_____

_____

_____

_____

_____

Did YOU meet your mindset & focus goals for this event?
Were you more or less focused and mindful than you anticipated? What helped or hindered your state of mind at this event *that you have control over and can improve upon?*

_____

_____

_____

_____

_____

Event Date/s:

Event Name and Type:

Event Location:

Dog/s Entered:

PRE EVENT PLANNING

What are your performance goals, for you & your dog?

_____
_____
_____
_____
_____

What are your mindset & focus goals for this event?

_____
_____
_____
_____
_____

POST EVENT EVALUATION & REFLECTION

Did YOU meet your performance goals for this event?
What skills were stronger than you anticipated? What skills were weaker than you anticipated? What helped or hindered your performance at this event *that you have control over & can improve upon?*

_____
_____
_____

_____
_____
_____
_____

Did your DOG meet your performance goals for this event?
Evaluate whether or not your dog met your performance goals for this event. What skills were stronger than you anticipated? What skills were weaker than you anticipated? What helped or hindered your dog's performance at this event *that you have control over and can improve upon?*

_____
_____
_____
_____
_____
_____

Did YOU meet your mindset & focus goals for this event?
Were you more or less focused and mindful than you anticipated? What helped or hindered your state of mind at this event *that you have control over and can improve upon?*

_____
_____
_____
_____
_____
_____

Event Date/s:

Event Name and Type:

Event Location:

Dog/s Entered:

PRE EVENT PLANNING
What are your performance goals, for you & your dog?

_____

_____

_____

_____

_____

What are your mindset & focus goals for this event?

_____

_____

_____

_____

_____

POST EVENT EVALUATION & REFLECTION
Did YOU meet your performance goals for this event?
What skills were stronger than you anticipated? What skills were weaker than you anticipated? What helped or hindered your performance at this event *that you have control over & can improve upon?*

_____

_____

_____

_____

_____

_____

_____

_____

Did your DOG meet your performance goals for this event?
Evaluate whether or not your dog met your performance goals for this event. What skills were stronger than you anticipated? What skills were weaker than you anticipated? What helped or hindered your dog's performance at this event *that you have control over and can improve upon?*

_____

_____

_____

_____

_____

_____

Did YOU meet your mindset & focus goals for this event?
Were you more or less focused and mindful than you anticipated? What helped or hindered your state of mind at this event *that you have control over and can improve upon?*

_____

_____

_____

_____

_____

Event Date/s:

Event Name and Type:

Event Location:

Dog/s Entered:

PRE EVENT PLANNING
What are your performance goals, for you & your dog?

_____

_____

_____

_____

_____

What are your mindset & focus goals for this event?

_____

_____

_____

_____

_____

POST EVENT EVALUATION & REFLECTION
Did YOU meet your performance goals for this event?
What skills were stronger than you anticipated? What skills were weaker than you anticipated? What helped or hindered your performance at this event *that you have control over & can improve upon?*

_____

_____

_____

_____

_____

_____

_____

Did your DOG meet your performance goals for this event?
Evaluate whether or not your dog met your performance goals for this event. What skills were stronger than you anticipated? What skills were weaker than you anticipated? What helped or hindered your dog's performance at this event *that you have control over and can improve upon?*

_____

_____

_____

_____

_____

_____

Did YOU meet your mindset & focus goals for this event?
Were you more or less focused and mindful than you anticipated? What helped or hindered your state of mind at this event *that you have control over and can improve upon?*

_____

_____

_____

_____

_____

Training Session Tracker

The following sheets are for keeping track of your training sessions. They're designed to help you maximize your training time with your dog, while minimizing frustration and confusion.

For Every Training Session:

1. You need to establish a (reachable) **specific goal**. Vague overall performance targets like 'succeed' or 'get better' won't cut it. *Write down your goal for each training session in this journal before heading out to train!*

2. You must be maximally **focused** on improvement during practice. It must be intense, uninterrupted and at least somewhat repetitive ('drilling'). Not always particularly pleasant, but highly rewarding. It's also critical that you make deliberate practice rewarding for your dog, which means you will potentially need to break things down in to

---

Be sure to make it worthwhile for your dog to play your the game!

---

very small and rewardable pieces that you can repeat for additional reinforcement!
3. You must receive **immediate feedback** on your performance. Without it, you can't figure out what you need to modify or how close you are to achieving your specific goal. Luckily, although many of us train alone, we always have our dog available to give us that immediate feedback!
4. You must **get out of your comfort zone**, constantly attempting things that are just out of reach. Ideally, you'll feel uncomfortable - *the whole time*.

A hallmark of deliberate practice is that performance level during training is not initially at the desired level – there is a gap. ***By the end of each training session, there should be something measurable that you or your dog has improved on.***

Embracing these principles in training squeezes the trigger of the greatest weapon in the arsenal of the human brain – adaptability.

DATE:

TOPIC / GOAL & CRITERIA FOR SUCCESS:

WHAT PROGRESS DID YOU MAKE? Did you meet your established criteria?

WHAT NEEDS TO BE WORKED ON FOR NEXT TIME?

TRAINING IS ALL ABOUT MAKING DECISIONS

NOTES / QUESTIONS:

DATE:

TOPIC / GOAL & CRITERIA FOR SUCCESS:

WHAT PROGRESS DID YOU MAKE? Did you meet your established criteria?

WHAT NEEDS TO BE WORKED ON FOR NEXT TIME?

BE A SPLITTER, NOT A LUMPER

NOTES / QUESTIONS:

DATE:

TOPIC / GOAL & CRITERIA FOR SUCCESS:

WHAT PROGRESS DID YOU MAKE? Did you meet your established criteria?

WHAT NEEDS TO BE WORKED ON FOR NEXT TIME?

TALENT IS A MYTH

NOTES / QUESTIONS:

DATE:

TOPIC / GOAL & CRITERIA FOR SUCCESS:

WHAT PROGRESS DID YOU MAKE? Did you meet your established criteria?

WHAT NEEDS TO BE WORKED ON FOR NEXT TIME?

MAKE IT WORTHWHILE FOR YOUR DOG TO PLAY THE GAME WITH YOU!

NOTES / QUESTIONS:

DATE:

TOPIC / GOAL & CRITERIA FOR SUCCESS:

WHAT PROGRESS DID YOU MAKE? Did you meet your established criteria?

WHAT NEEDS TO BE WORKED ON FOR NEXT TIME?

THINK, PLAN, DO, REVIEW

NOTES / QUESTIONS:

DATE:

TOPIC / GOAL & CRITERIA FOR SUCCESS:

WHAT PROGRESS DID YOU MAKE? Did you meet your established criteria?

WHAT NEEDS TO BE WORKED ON FOR NEXT TIME?

YOU GET WHAT YOU REINFORCE

NOTES / QUESTIONS:

DATE:

TOPIC / GOAL & CRITERIA FOR SUCCESS:

WHAT PROGRESS DID YOU MAKE? Did you meet your established criteria?

WHAT NEEDS TO BE WORKED ON FOR NEXT TIME?

IF YOU'RE NOT FAILING, YOU'RE NOT GROWING

NOTES / QUESTIONS:

DATE:

TOPIC / GOAL & CRITERIA FOR SUCCESS:

WHAT PROGRESS DID YOU MAKE? Did you meet your established criteria?

WHAT NEEDS TO BE WORKED ON FOR NEXT TIME?

BE PRESENT FOR YOUR PRACTICE

NOTES / QUESTIONS:

DATE:

TOPIC / GOAL & CRITERIA FOR SUCCESS:

WHAT PROGRESS DID YOU MAKE? Did you meet your established criteria?

WHAT NEEDS TO BE WORKED ON FOR NEXT TIME?

PRACTICE UNTIL YOU CAN'T GET IT WRONG

NOTES / QUESTIONS:

DATE:

TOPIC / GOAL & CRITERIA FOR SUCCESS:

WHAT PROGRESS DID YOU MAKE? Did you meet your established criteria?

WHAT NEEDS TO BE WORKED ON FOR NEXT TIME?

TRAINING IS ALL ABOUT MAKING DECISIONS

NOTES / QUESTIONS:

DATE:

TOPIC / GOAL & CRITERIA FOR SUCCESS:

WHAT PROGRESS DID YOU MAKE? Did you meet your established criteria?

WHAT NEEDS TO BE WORKED ON FOR NEXT TIME?

BE A SPLITTER, NOT A LUMPER

NOTES / QUESTIONS:

RATE YOUR MINDSET
★★★★★

RATE YOUR MECHANICS
★★★★★

DATE:

TOPIC / GOAL & CRITERIA FOR SUCCESS:

WHAT PROGRESS DID YOU MAKE? Did you meet your established criteria?

WHAT NEEDS TO BE WORKED ON FOR NEXT TIME?

TALENT IS A MYTH

NOTES / QUESTIONS:

DATE:

TOPIC / GOAL & CRITERIA FOR SUCCESS:

WHAT PROGRESS DID YOU MAKE? Did you meet your established criteria?

WHAT NEEDS TO BE WORKED ON FOR NEXT TIME?

MAKE IT WORTHWHILE FOR YOUR DOG TO PLAY THE GAME WITH YOU!

NOTES / QUESTIONS:

DATE:

TOPIC / GOAL & CRITERIA FOR SUCCESS:

WHAT PROGRESS DID YOU MAKE? Did you meet your established criteria?

WHAT NEEDS TO BE WORKED ON FOR NEXT TIME?

THINK, PLAN, DO, REVIEW

NOTES / QUESTIONS:

DATE:

TOPIC / GOAL & CRITERIA FOR SUCCESS:

WHAT PROGRESS DID YOU MAKE? Did you meet your established criteria?

WHAT NEEDS TO BE WORKED ON FOR NEXT TIME?

YOU GET WHAT YOU REINFORCE

NOTES / QUESTIONS:

DATE:

TOPIC / GOAL & CRITERIA FOR SUCCESS:

WHAT PROGRESS DID YOU MAKE? Did you meet your established criteria?

WHAT NEEDS TO BE WORKED ON FOR NEXT TIME?

IF YOU'RE NOT FAILING, YOU'RE NOT GROWING

NOTES / QUESTIONS:

DATE:

TOPIC / GOAL & CRITERIA FOR SUCCESS:

WHAT PROGRESS DID YOU MAKE? Did you meet your established criteria?

WHAT NEEDS TO BE WORKED ON FOR NEXT TIME?

BE PRESENT FOR YOUR PRACTICE

NOTES / QUESTIONS:

DATE:

TOPIC / GOAL & CRITERIA FOR SUCCESS:

WHAT PROGRESS DID YOU MAKE? Did you meet your established criteria?

WHAT NEEDS TO BE WORKED ON FOR NEXT TIME?

PRACTICE UNTIL YOU CAN'T GET IT WRONG

NOTES / QUESTIONS:

DATE:

TOPIC / GOAL & CRITERIA FOR SUCCESS:

WHAT PROGRESS DID YOU MAKE? Did you meet your established criteria?

WHAT NEEDS TO BE WORKED ON FOR NEXT TIME?

TRAINING IS ALL ABOUT MAKING DECISIONS

NOTES / QUESTIONS:

DATE:

TOPIC / GOAL & CRITERIA FOR SUCCESS:

WHAT PROGRESS DID YOU MAKE? Did you meet your established criteria?

WHAT NEEDS TO BE WORKED ON FOR NEXT TIME?

BE A SPLITTER, NOT A LUMPER

NOTES / QUESTIONS:

DATE:

TOPIC / GOAL & CRITERIA FOR SUCCESS:

WHAT PROGRESS DID YOU MAKE? Did you meet your established criteria?

WHAT NEEDS TO BE WORKED ON FOR NEXT TIME?

TALENT IS A MYTH

NOTES / QUESTIONS:

DATE:

TOPIC / GOAL & CRITERIA FOR SUCCESS:

WHAT PROGRESS DID YOU MAKE? Did you meet your established criteria?

WHAT NEEDS TO BE WORKED ON FOR NEXT TIME?

MAKE IT WORTHWHILE FOR YOUR DOG TO PLAY THE GAME WITH YOU!

NOTES / QUESTIONS:

DATE:

TOPIC / GOAL & CRITERIA FOR SUCCESS:

WHAT PROGRESS DID YOU MAKE? Did you meet your established criteria?

WHAT NEEDS TO BE WORKED ON FOR NEXT TIME?

THINK, PLAN, DO, REVIEW

NOTES / QUESTIONS:

DATE:

TOPIC / GOAL & CRITERIA FOR SUCCESS:

WHAT PROGRESS DID YOU MAKE? Did you meet your established criteria?

WHAT NEEDS TO BE WORKED ON FOR NEXT TIME?

YOU GET WHAT YOU REINFORCE

NOTES / QUESTIONS:

DATE:

TOPIC / GOAL & CRITERIA FOR SUCCESS:

WHAT PROGRESS DID YOU MAKE? Did you meet your established criteria?

WHAT NEEDS TO BE WORKED ON FOR NEXT TIME?

IF YOU'RE NOT FAILING, YOU'RE NOT GROWING

NOTES / QUESTIONS:

DATE:

TOPIC / GOAL & CRITERIA FOR SUCCESS:

WHAT PROGRESS DID YOU MAKE? Did you meet your established criteria?

WHAT NEEDS TO BE WORKED ON FOR NEXT TIME?

BE PRESENT FOR YOUR PRACTICE

NOTES / QUESTIONS:

DATE:

TOPIC / GOAL & CRITERIA FOR SUCCESS:

WHAT PROGRESS DID YOU MAKE? Did you meet your established criteria?

WHAT NEEDS TO BE WORKED ON FOR NEXT TIME?

PRACTICE UNTIL YOU CAN'T GET IT WRONG

NOTES / QUESTIONS:

DATE:

TOPIC / GOAL & CRITERIA FOR SUCCESS:

WHAT PROGRESS DID YOU MAKE? Did you meet your established criteria?

WHAT NEEDS TO BE WORKED ON FOR NEXT TIME?

TRAINING IS ALL ABOUT MAKING DECISIONS

NOTES / QUESTIONS:

DATE:

TOPIC / GOAL & CRITERIA FOR SUCCESS:

WHAT PROGRESS DID YOU MAKE? Did you meet your established criteria?

WHAT NEEDS TO BE WORKED ON FOR NEXT TIME?

BE A SPLITTER, NOT A LUMPER

NOTES / QUESTIONS:

DATE:

TOPIC / GOAL & CRITERIA FOR SUCCESS:

WHAT PROGRESS DID YOU MAKE? Did you meet your established criteria?

WHAT NEEDS TO BE WORKED ON FOR NEXT TIME?

TALENT IS A MYTH

NOTES / QUESTIONS:

DATE:

TOPIC / GOAL & CRITERIA FOR SUCCESS:

WHAT PROGRESS DID YOU MAKE? Did you meet your established criteria?

WHAT NEEDS TO BE WORKED ON FOR NEXT TIME?

MAKE IT WORTHWHILE FOR YOUR DOG TO PLAY THE GAME WITH YOU!

NOTES / QUESTIONS:

DATE:

TOPIC / GOAL & CRITERIA FOR SUCCESS:

WHAT PROGRESS DID YOU MAKE? Did you meet your established criteria?

WHAT NEEDS TO BE WORKED ON FOR NEXT TIME?

THINK, PLAN, DO, REVIEW

NOTES / QUESTIONS:

DATE:

TOPIC / GOAL & CRITERIA FOR SUCCESS:

WHAT PROGRESS DID YOU MAKE? Did you meet your established criteria?

WHAT NEEDS TO BE WORKED ON FOR NEXT TIME?

YOU GET WHAT YOU REINFORCE

NOTES / QUESTIONS:

DATE:

TOPIC / GOAL & CRITERIA FOR SUCCESS:

WHAT PROGRESS DID YOU MAKE? Did you meet your established criteria?

WHAT NEEDS TO BE WORKED ON FOR NEXT TIME?

IF YOU'RE NOT FAILING, YOU'RE NOT GROWING

NOTES / QUESTIONS:

DATE:

TOPIC / GOAL & CRITERIA FOR SUCCESS:

WHAT PROGRESS DID YOU MAKE? Did you meet your established criteria?

WHAT NEEDS TO BE WORKED ON FOR NEXT TIME?

BE PRESENT FOR YOUR PRACTICE

NOTES / QUESTIONS:

DATE:

TOPIC / GOAL & CRITERIA FOR SUCCESS:

WHAT PROGRESS DID YOU MAKE? Did you meet your established criteria?

WHAT NEEDS TO BE WORKED ON FOR NEXT TIME?

PRACTICE UNTIL YOU CAN'T GET IT WRONG

NOTES / QUESTIONS:

DATE:

TOPIC / GOAL & CRITERIA FOR SUCCESS:

WHAT PROGRESS DID YOU MAKE? Did you meet your established criteria?

WHAT NEEDS TO BE WORKED ON FOR NEXT TIME?

TRAINING IS ALL ABOUT MAKING DECISIONS

NOTES / QUESTIONS:

DATE:

TOPIC / GOAL & CRITERIA FOR SUCCESS:

WHAT PROGRESS DID YOU MAKE? Did you meet your established criteria?

WHAT NEEDS TO BE WORKED ON FOR NEXT TIME?

BE A SPLITTER, NOT A LUMPER

NOTES / QUESTIONS:

DATE:

TOPIC / GOAL & CRITERIA FOR SUCCESS:

WHAT PROGRESS DID YOU MAKE? Did you meet your established criteria?

WHAT NEEDS TO BE WORKED ON FOR NEXT TIME?

TALENT IS A MYTH

NOTES / QUESTIONS:

DATE:

TOPIC / GOAL & CRITERIA FOR SUCCESS:

WHAT PROGRESS DID YOU MAKE? Did you meet your established criteria?

WHAT NEEDS TO BE WORKED ON FOR NEXT TIME?

MAKE IT WORTHWHILE FOR YOUR DOG TO PLAY THE GAME WITH YOU!

NOTES / QUESTIONS:

DATE:

TOPIC / GOAL & CRITERIA FOR SUCCESS:

WHAT PROGRESS DID YOU MAKE? Did you meet your established criteria?

WHAT NEEDS TO BE WORKED ON FOR NEXT TIME?

THINK, PLAN, DO, REVIEW

NOTES / QUESTIONS:

DATE:

TOPIC / GOAL & CRITERIA FOR SUCCESS:

WHAT PROGRESS DID YOU MAKE? Did you meet your established criteria?

WHAT NEEDS TO BE WORKED ON FOR NEXT TIME?

YOU GET WHAT YOU REINFORCE

NOTES / QUESTIONS:

DATE:

TOPIC / GOAL & CRITERIA FOR SUCCESS:

WHAT PROGRESS DID YOU MAKE? Did you meet your established criteria?

WHAT NEEDS TO BE WORKED ON FOR NEXT TIME?

IF YOU'RE NOT FAILING, YOU'RE NOT GROWING

NOTES / QUESTIONS:

DATE:

TOPIC / GOAL & CRITERIA FOR SUCCESS:

WHAT PROGRESS DID YOU MAKE? Did you meet your established criteria?

WHAT NEEDS TO BE WORKED ON FOR NEXT TIME?

BE PRESENT FOR YOUR PRACTICE

NOTES / QUESTIONS:

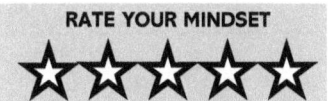

DATE:

TOPIC / GOAL & CRITERIA FOR SUCCESS:

WHAT PROGRESS DID YOU MAKE? Did you meet your established criteria?

WHAT NEEDS TO BE WORKED ON FOR NEXT TIME?

PRACTICE UNTIL YOU CAN'T GET IT WRONG

NOTES / QUESTIONS:

DATE:

TOPIC / GOAL & CRITERIA FOR SUCCESS:

WHAT PROGRESS DID YOU MAKE? Did you meet your established criteria?

WHAT NEEDS TO BE WORKED ON FOR NEXT TIME?

TRAINING IS ALL ABOUT MAKING DECISIONS

NOTES / QUESTIONS:

DATE:

TOPIC / GOAL & CRITERIA FOR SUCCESS:

WHAT PROGRESS DID YOU MAKE? Did you meet your established criteria?

WHAT NEEDS TO BE WORKED ON FOR NEXT TIME?

BE A SPLITTER, NOT A LUMPER

NOTES / QUESTIONS:

RATE YOUR MINDSET
☆☆☆☆☆

RATE YOUR MECHANICS
☆☆☆☆☆

DATE:

TOPIC / GOAL & CRITERIA FOR SUCCESS:

WHAT PROGRESS DID YOU MAKE? Did you meet your established criteria?

WHAT NEEDS TO BE WORKED ON FOR NEXT TIME?

TALENT IS A MYTH

NOTES / QUESTIONS:

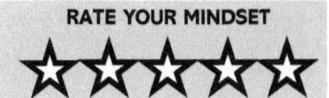

DATE:

TOPIC / GOAL & CRITERIA FOR SUCCESS:

WHAT PROGRESS DID YOU MAKE? Did you meet your established criteria?

WHAT NEEDS TO BE WORKED ON FOR NEXT TIME?

MAKE IT WORTHWHILE FOR YOUR DOG TO PLAY THE GAME WITH YOU!

NOTES / QUESTIONS:

DATE:

TOPIC / GOAL & CRITERIA FOR SUCCESS:

WHAT PROGRESS DID YOU MAKE? Did you meet your established criteria?

WHAT NEEDS TO BE WORKED ON FOR NEXT TIME?

THINK, PLAN, DO, REVIEW

NOTES / QUESTIONS:

RATE YOUR MINDSET
☆☆☆☆☆

RATE YOUR MECHANICS
☆☆☆☆☆

DATE:

TOPIC / GOAL & CRITERIA FOR SUCCESS:

WHAT PROGRESS DID YOU MAKE? Did you meet your established criteria?

WHAT NEEDS TO BE WORKED ON FOR NEXT TIME?

YOU GET WHAT YOU REINFORCE

NOTES / QUESTIONS:

RATE YOUR MINDSET
☆☆☆☆☆

RATE YOUR MECHANICS
☆☆☆☆☆

DATE:

TOPIC / GOAL & CRITERIA FOR SUCCESS:

WHAT PROGRESS DID YOU MAKE? Did you meet your established criteria?

WHAT NEEDS TO BE WORKED ON FOR NEXT TIME?

IF YOU'RE NOT FAILING, YOU'RE NOT GROWING

NOTES / QUESTIONS:

DATE:

TOPIC / GOAL & CRITERIA FOR SUCCESS:

WHAT PROGRESS DID YOU MAKE? Did you meet your established criteria?

WHAT NEEDS TO BE WORKED ON FOR NEXT TIME?

BE PRESENT FOR YOUR PRACTICE

NOTES / QUESTIONS:

DATE:

TOPIC / GOAL & CRITERIA FOR SUCCESS:

WHAT PROGRESS DID YOU MAKE? Did you meet your established criteria?

WHAT NEEDS TO BE WORKED ON FOR NEXT TIME?

PRACTICE UNTIL YOU CAN'T GET IT WRONG

NOTES / QUESTIONS:

DATE:

TOPIC / GOAL & CRITERIA FOR SUCCESS:

WHAT PROGRESS DID YOU MAKE? Did you meet your established criteria?

WHAT NEEDS TO BE WORKED ON FOR NEXT TIME?

TRAINING IS ALL ABOUT MAKING DECISIONS

NOTES / QUESTIONS:

DATE:

TOPIC / GOAL & CRITERIA FOR SUCCESS:

WHAT PROGRESS DID YOU MAKE? Did you meet your established criteria?

WHAT NEEDS TO BE WORKED ON FOR NEXT TIME?

BE A SPLITTER, NOT A LUMPER

NOTES / QUESTIONS:

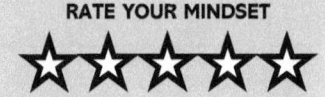

DATE:

TOPIC / GOAL & CRITERIA FOR SUCCESS:

WHAT PROGRESS DID YOU MAKE? Did you meet your established criteria?

WHAT NEEDS TO BE WORKED ON FOR NEXT TIME?

TALENT IS A MYTH

NOTES / QUESTIONS:

DATE:

TOPIC / GOAL & CRITERIA FOR SUCCESS:

WHAT PROGRESS DID YOU MAKE? Did you meet your established criteria?

WHAT NEEDS TO BE WORKED ON FOR NEXT TIME?

MAKE IT WORTHWHILE FOR YOUR DOG TO PLAY THE GAME WITH YOU!

NOTES / QUESTIONS:

DATE:

TOPIC / GOAL & CRITERIA FOR SUCCESS:

WHAT PROGRESS DID YOU MAKE? Did you meet your established criteria?

WHAT NEEDS TO BE WORKED ON FOR NEXT TIME?

THINK, PLAN, DO, REVIEW

NOTES / QUESTIONS:

DATE:

TOPIC / GOAL & CRITERIA FOR SUCCESS:

WHAT PROGRESS DID YOU MAKE? Did you meet your established criteria?

WHAT NEEDS TO BE WORKED ON FOR NEXT TIME?

YOU GET WHAT YOU REINFORCE

NOTES / QUESTIONS:

RATE YOUR MINDSET
☆☆☆☆☆

RATE YOUR MECHANICS
☆☆☆☆☆

DATE:

TOPIC / GOAL & CRITERIA FOR SUCCESS:

WHAT PROGRESS DID YOU MAKE? Did you meet your established criteria?

WHAT NEEDS TO BE WORKED ON FOR NEXT TIME?

IF YOU'RE NOT FAILING, YOU'RE NOT GROWING

NOTES / QUESTIONS:

DATE:

TOPIC / GOAL & CRITERIA FOR SUCCESS:

WHAT PROGRESS DID YOU MAKE? Did you meet your established criteria?

WHAT NEEDS TO BE WORKED ON FOR NEXT TIME?

BE PRESENT FOR YOUR PRACTICE

NOTES / QUESTIONS:

DATE:

TOPIC / GOAL & CRITERIA FOR SUCCESS:

WHAT PROGRESS DID YOU MAKE? Did you meet your established criteria?

WHAT NEEDS TO BE WORKED ON FOR NEXT TIME?

PRACTICE UNTIL YOU CAN'T GET IT WRONG

NOTES / QUESTIONS:

DATE:

TOPIC / GOAL & CRITERIA FOR SUCCESS:

WHAT PROGRESS DID YOU MAKE? Did you meet your established criteria?

WHAT NEEDS TO BE WORKED ON FOR NEXT TIME?

TRAINING IS ALL ABOUT MAKING DECISIONS

NOTES / QUESTIONS:

DATE:

TOPIC / GOAL & CRITERIA FOR SUCCESS:

WHAT PROGRESS DID YOU MAKE? Did you meet your established criteria?

WHAT NEEDS TO BE WORKED ON FOR NEXT TIME?

BE A SPLITTER, NOT A LUMPER

NOTES / QUESTIONS:

DATE:

TOPIC / GOAL & CRITERIA FOR SUCCESS:

WHAT PROGRESS DID YOU MAKE? Did you meet your established criteria?

WHAT NEEDS TO BE WORKED ON FOR NEXT TIME?

TALENT IS A MYTH

NOTES / QUESTIONS:

RATE YOUR MINDSET
☆☆☆☆☆

RATE YOUR MECHANICS
☆☆☆☆☆

DATE:

TOPIC / GOAL & CRITERIA FOR SUCCESS:

WHAT PROGRESS DID YOU MAKE? Did you meet your established criteria?

WHAT NEEDS TO BE WORKED ON FOR NEXT TIME?

MAKE IT WORTHWHILE FOR YOUR DOG TO PLAY THE GAME WITH YOU!

NOTES / QUESTIONS:

DATE:

TOPIC / GOAL & CRITERIA FOR SUCCESS:

WHAT PROGRESS DID YOU MAKE? Did you meet your established criteria?

WHAT NEEDS TO BE WORKED ON FOR NEXT TIME?

THINK, PLAN, DO, REVIEW

NOTES / QUESTIONS:

DATE:

TOPIC / GOAL & CRITERIA FOR SUCCESS:

WHAT PROGRESS DID YOU MAKE? Did you meet your established criteria?

WHAT NEEDS TO BE WORKED ON FOR NEXT TIME?

YOU GET WHAT YOU REINFORCE

NOTES / QUESTIONS:

DATE:

TOPIC / GOAL & CRITERIA FOR SUCCESS:

WHAT PROGRESS DID YOU MAKE? Did you meet your established criteria?

WHAT NEEDS TO BE WORKED ON FOR NEXT TIME?

IF YOU'RE NOT FAILING, YOU'RE NOT GROWING

NOTES / QUESTIONS:

DATE:

TOPIC / GOAL & CRITERIA FOR SUCCESS:

WHAT PROGRESS DID YOU MAKE? Did you meet your established criteria?

WHAT NEEDS TO BE WORKED ON FOR NEXT TIME?

BE PRESENT FOR YOUR PRACTICE

NOTES / QUESTIONS:

DATE:

TOPIC / GOAL & CRITERIA FOR SUCCESS:

WHAT PROGRESS DID YOU MAKE? Did you meet your established criteria?

WHAT NEEDS TO BE WORKED ON FOR NEXT TIME?

PRACTICE UNTIL YOU CAN'T GET IT WRONG

NOTES / QUESTIONS:

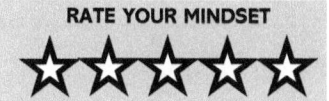

DATE:

TOPIC / GOAL & CRITERIA FOR SUCCESS:

WHAT PROGRESS DID YOU MAKE? Did you meet your established criteria?

WHAT NEEDS TO BE WORKED ON FOR NEXT TIME?

TRAINING IS ALL ABOUT MAKING DECISIONS

NOTES / QUESTIONS:

DATE:

TOPIC / GOAL & CRITERIA FOR SUCCESS:

WHAT PROGRESS DID YOU MAKE? Did you meet your established criteria?

WHAT NEEDS TO BE WORKED ON FOR NEXT TIME?

BE A SPLITTER, NOT A LUMPER

NOTES / QUESTIONS:

DATE:

TOPIC / GOAL & CRITERIA FOR SUCCESS:

WHAT PROGRESS DID YOU MAKE? Did you meet your established criteria?

WHAT NEEDS TO BE WORKED ON FOR NEXT TIME?

TALENT IS A MYTH

NOTES / QUESTIONS:

DATE:

TOPIC / GOAL & CRITERIA FOR SUCCESS:

WHAT PROGRESS DID YOU MAKE? Did you meet your established criteria?

WHAT NEEDS TO BE WORKED ON FOR NEXT TIME?

MAKE IT WORTHWHILE FOR YOUR DOG TO PLAY THE GAME WITH YOU!

NOTES / QUESTIONS:

DATE:

TOPIC / GOAL & CRITERIA FOR SUCCESS:

WHAT PROGRESS DID YOU MAKE? Did you meet your established criteria?

WHAT NEEDS TO BE WORKED ON FOR NEXT TIME?

THINK, PLAN, DO, REVIEW

NOTES / QUESTIONS:

DATE:

TOPIC / GOAL & CRITERIA FOR SUCCESS:

WHAT PROGRESS DID YOU MAKE? Did you meet your established criteria?

WHAT NEEDS TO BE WORKED ON FOR NEXT TIME?

YOU GET WHAT YOU REINFORCE

NOTES / QUESTIONS:

RATE YOUR MINDSET
☆☆☆☆☆

RATE YOUR MECHANICS
☆☆☆☆☆

DATE:

TOPIC / GOAL & CRITERIA FOR SUCCESS:

WHAT PROGRESS DID YOU MAKE? Did you meet your established criteria?

WHAT NEEDS TO BE WORKED ON FOR NEXT TIME?

IF YOU'RE NOT FAILING, YOU'RE NOT GROWING

NOTES / QUESTIONS:

DATE:

TOPIC / GOAL & CRITERIA FOR SUCCESS:

WHAT PROGRESS DID YOU MAKE? Did you meet your established criteria?

WHAT NEEDS TO BE WORKED ON FOR NEXT TIME?

BE PRESENT FOR YOUR PRACTICE

NOTES / QUESTIONS:

DATE:

TOPIC / GOAL & CRITERIA FOR SUCCESS:

WHAT PROGRESS DID YOU MAKE? Did you meet your established criteria?

WHAT NEEDS TO BE WORKED ON FOR NEXT TIME?

PRACTICE UNTIL YOU CAN'T GET IT WRONG

NOTES / QUESTIONS:

DATE:

TOPIC / GOAL & CRITERIA FOR SUCCESS:

WHAT PROGRESS DID YOU MAKE? Did you meet your established criteria?

WHAT NEEDS TO BE WORKED ON FOR NEXT TIME?

TRAINING IS ALL ABOUT MAKING DECISIONS

NOTES / QUESTIONS:

DATE:

TOPIC / GOAL & CRITERIA FOR SUCCESS:

WHAT PROGRESS DID YOU MAKE? Did you meet your established criteria?

WHAT NEEDS TO BE WORKED ON FOR NEXT TIME?

BE A SPLITTER, NOT A LUMPER

NOTES / QUESTIONS:

RATE YOUR MINDSET

RATE YOUR MECHANICS

DATE:

TOPIC / GOAL & CRITERIA FOR SUCCESS:

WHAT PROGRESS DID YOU MAKE? Did you meet your established criteria?

WHAT NEEDS TO BE WORKED ON FOR NEXT TIME?

TALENT IS A MYTH

NOTES / QUESTIONS:

DATE:

TOPIC / GOAL & CRITERIA FOR SUCCESS:

WHAT PROGRESS DID YOU MAKE? Did you meet your established criteria?

WHAT NEEDS TO BE WORKED ON FOR NEXT TIME?

MAKE IT WORTHWHILE FOR YOUR DOG TO PLAY THE GAME WITH YOU!

NOTES / QUESTIONS:

DATE:

TOPIC / GOAL & CRITERIA FOR SUCCESS:

WHAT PROGRESS DID YOU MAKE? Did you meet your established criteria?

WHAT NEEDS TO BE WORKED ON FOR NEXT TIME?

THINK, PLAN, DO, REVIEW

NOTES / QUESTIONS:

DATE:

TOPIC / GOAL & CRITERIA FOR SUCCESS:

WHAT PROGRESS DID YOU MAKE? Did you meet your established criteria?

WHAT NEEDS TO BE WORKED ON FOR NEXT TIME?

YOU GET WHAT YOU REINFORCE

NOTES / QUESTIONS:

RATE YOUR MINDSET
☆☆☆☆☆

RATE YOUR MECHANICS
☆☆☆☆☆

DATE:

TOPIC / GOAL & CRITERIA FOR SUCCESS:

WHAT PROGRESS DID YOU MAKE? Did you meet your established criteria?

WHAT NEEDS TO BE WORKED ON FOR NEXT TIME?

IF YOU'RE NOT FAILING, YOU'RE NOT GROWING

NOTES / QUESTIONS:

DATE:

TOPIC / GOAL & CRITERIA FOR SUCCESS:

WHAT PROGRESS DID YOU MAKE? Did you meet your established criteria?

WHAT NEEDS TO BE WORKED ON FOR NEXT TIME?

BE PRESENT FOR YOUR PRACTICE

NOTES / QUESTIONS:

DATE:

TOPIC / GOAL & CRITERIA FOR SUCCESS:

WHAT PROGRESS DID YOU MAKE? Did you meet your established criteria?

WHAT NEEDS TO BE WORKED ON FOR NEXT TIME?

PRACTICE UNTIL YOU CAN'T GET IT WRONG

NOTES / QUESTIONS:

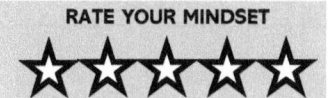

DATE:

TOPIC / GOAL & CRITERIA FOR SUCCESS:

WHAT PROGRESS DID YOU MAKE? Did you meet your established criteria?

WHAT NEEDS TO BE WORKED ON FOR NEXT TIME?

TRAINING IS ALL ABOUT MAKING DECISIONS

NOTES / QUESTIONS:

DATE:

TOPIC / GOAL & CRITERIA FOR SUCCESS:

WHAT PROGRESS DID YOU MAKE? Did you meet your established criteria?

WHAT NEEDS TO BE WORKED ON FOR NEXT TIME?

BE A SPLITTER, NOT A LUMPER

NOTES / QUESTIONS:

DATE:

TOPIC / GOAL & CRITERIA FOR SUCCESS:

WHAT PROGRESS DID YOU MAKE? Did you meet your established criteria?

WHAT NEEDS TO BE WORKED ON FOR NEXT TIME?

TALENT IS A MYTH

NOTES / QUESTIONS:

DATE:

TOPIC / GOAL & CRITERIA FOR SUCCESS:

WHAT PROGRESS DID YOU MAKE? Did you meet your established criteria?

WHAT NEEDS TO BE WORKED ON FOR NEXT TIME?

MAKE IT WORTHWHILE FOR YOUR DOG TO PLAY THE GAME WITH YOU!

NOTES / QUESTIONS:

DATE:

TOPIC / GOAL & CRITERIA FOR SUCCESS:

WHAT PROGRESS DID YOU MAKE? Did you meet your established criteria?

WHAT NEEDS TO BE WORKED ON FOR NEXT TIME?

THINK, PLAN, DO, REVIEW

NOTES / QUESTIONS:

DATE:

TOPIC / GOAL & CRITERIA FOR SUCCESS:

WHAT PROGRESS DID YOU MAKE? Did you meet your established criteria?

WHAT NEEDS TO BE WORKED ON FOR NEXT TIME?

YOU GET WHAT YOU REINFORCE

NOTES / QUESTIONS:

RATE YOUR MINDSET
☆☆☆☆☆

RATE YOUR MECHANICS
☆☆☆☆☆

DATE:

TOPIC / GOAL & CRITERIA FOR SUCCESS:

WHAT PROGRESS DID YOU MAKE? Did you meet your established criteria?

WHAT NEEDS TO BE WORKED ON FOR NEXT TIME?

IF YOU'RE NOT FAILING, YOU'RE NOT GROWING

NOTES / QUESTIONS:

DATE:

TOPIC / GOAL & CRITERIA FOR SUCCESS:

WHAT PROGRESS DID YOU MAKE? Did you meet your established criteria?

WHAT NEEDS TO BE WORKED ON FOR NEXT TIME?

BE PRESENT FOR YOUR PRACTICE

NOTES / QUESTIONS:

DATE:

TOPIC / GOAL & CRITERIA FOR SUCCESS:

WHAT PROGRESS DID YOU MAKE? Did you meet your established criteria?

WHAT NEEDS TO BE WORKED ON FOR NEXT TIME?

PRACTICE UNTIL YOU CAN'T GET IT WRONG

NOTES / QUESTIONS:

My To Do List

Your To Do List will constantly evolve! You may find that you check off things on your list as completed, only to circle back and find that you need to work on them again, and that's totally fine! Use your To Do List as well as previous training sessions to help decide just what to work on during your time with your dog!

- ☐
- ☐
- ☐
- ☐
- ☐
- ☐
- ☐
- ☐
- ☐
- ☐
- ☐
- ☐
- ☐
- ☐
- ☐
- ☐
- ☐
- ☐
- ☐

My To Do List

- [ ]
- [ ]
- [ ]
- [ ]
- [ ]
- [ ]
- [ ]
- [ ]
- [ ]
- [ ]
- [ ]
- [ ]
- [ ]
- [ ]
- [ ]
- [ ]
- [ ]
- [ ]
- [ ]
- [ ]
- [ ]
- [ ]
- [ ]
- [ ]
- [ ]
- [ ]
- [ ]
- [ ]
- [ ]
- [ ]

My To Do List

- [ ]
- [ ]
- [ ]
- [ ]
- [ ]
- [ ]
- [ ]
- [ ]
- [ ]
- [ ]
- [ ]
- [ ]
- [ ]
- [ ]
- [ ]
- [ ]
- [ ]
- [ ]
- [ ]
- [ ]
- [ ]
- [ ]
- [ ]
- [ ]
- [ ]
- [ ]
- [ ]
- [ ]
- [ ]
- [ ]

My To Do List

My To Do List

- [ ]
- [ ]
- [ ]
- [ ]
- [ ]
- [ ]
- [ ]
- [ ]
- [ ]
- [ ]
- [ ]
- [ ]
- [ ]
- [ ]
- [ ]
- [ ]
- [ ]
- [ ]
- [ ]
- [ ]
- [ ]
- [ ]
- [ ]
- [ ]
- [ ]
- [ ]
- [ ]
- [ ]
- [ ]
- [ ]
- [ ]

My To Do List

- [ ]
- [ ]
- [ ]
- [ ]
- [ ]
- [ ]
- [ ]
- [ ]
- [ ]
- [ ]
- [ ]
- [ ]
- [ ]
- [ ]
- [ ]
- [ ]
- [ ]
- [ ]
- [ ]
- [ ]
- [ ]
- [ ]
- [ ]
- [ ]
- [ ]
- [ ]
- [ ]
- [ ]
- [ ]
- [ ]

THE AGILITY CHALLENGE PURPOSEFUL PRACTICE TRAINING JOURNAL

BY
DAISY PEEL

LEARN MORE AT
WWW.THEAGILITYCHALLENGE.COM

www.ingramcontent.com/pod-product-compliance
Lightning Source LLC
Chambersburg PA
CBHW020902080526
44589CB00011B/402